STORIES OF ROME

KING ANCUS MARCIUS

ADAPTED FROM THE HISTORIES OF LIVY AND DIONYSIUS

SAM VANDERPLAS

LUCERNA

LUCERNA

This edition published in 2025 by Lucerna Press
Fort Worth, Texas

This work was developed with the assistance of artificial intelligence tools. The content reflects the author's intent and judgment.

ISBN: 979-8-218-72130-5

Printed in the United States of America

Tullus Hostilius, the third king of Rome, did not fear the gods. He cared only for battles and victories. He let the temples grow cold and quiet. The sacred fires burned low, and no prayers rose to heaven.

The people saw this and wondered. Some said it did not matter. Others were afraid.

One day, without warning, a thunderbolt came from the sky. It struck the king's palace and set it on fire. The walls burned. The roof fell. Tullus was gone.

Then the people knew: the gods had not forgotten. And they remembered the old kings who had walked in fear and wisdom.

After Tullus died, the Senate ruled for a time. But the people wanted a king who would bring peace, not pride. They chose a man named Ancus Marcius.

Ancus was the grandson of King Numa, who had loved the gods and taught the people to worship. But Ancus was also strong. He had learned from both Numa and Tullus.

He said, "A king must serve both heaven and earth. We will keep the rites of the gods, and we will guard the city."

So Ancus became the fourth king of Rome. The people hoped he would rule with both justice and strength.

The first thing Ancus did was to restore the worship of the gods. He called the priests together and told them, "Write down the sacred laws, so they will never be forgotten."

The temples were opened again. The altars were swept clean. The fires on the hearths were lit. Songs and prayers rose from the hills of Rome, just as they had in the days of King Numa.

The people watched and listened. Many had forgotten how to pray. But under Ancus, the old ways returned. The gods were honored once more.

But while Rome was turning back to the gods, her enemies were watching. The Latin tribes to the south said, "Rome has grown weak. This new king only cares for temples and prayers."

So they crossed the border. They stole cattle. They burned farms. They thought Rome would not fight back.

But they were wrong.

When news came to the city, Ancus gathered the people. He prayed at the altars and asked the gods to bless what was just. Then he sent a message: "We seek peace, but we are ready for war."

When Latin raiders crossed Rome's borders, Ancus declared that peace had been broken.

But the Romans could not go to war without first asking the gods. The priests were called—fetials, guardians of sacred war rites.

One stood at the border and spoke the ancient words, demanding justice. Thirty-three days passed in silence. At last, he took a spear tipped with iron and cast it into enemy land.

Only then did the king summon the army. The soldiers marched with banners raised and the favor of the gods upon them.

Ancus led Rome's army against the Latin cities. They fought at Politorium, Tellenae, and Ficana, towns that had once stood proud.

Now their walls lay in ruins. Their temples stood empty. Their people were taken captive. Some cities were erased completely, leveled to dust and stone.

The survivors were not left to wander. Ancus gave them land on the Aventine Hill and brought them into Rome.

Through conquest, Rome became strong.

The Tiber River flowed through the middle of Rome. On one side were the Palatine and Aventine Hills. On the other stood the Janiculum, high and wide.

But there was no bridge.

People crossed the river in boats. Soldiers had to wait for rafts. If enemies came from beyond the river, Rome would not be ready.

Ancus saw this, and he knew what must be done. "A city divided cannot last," he said. "We must bind the two sides together."

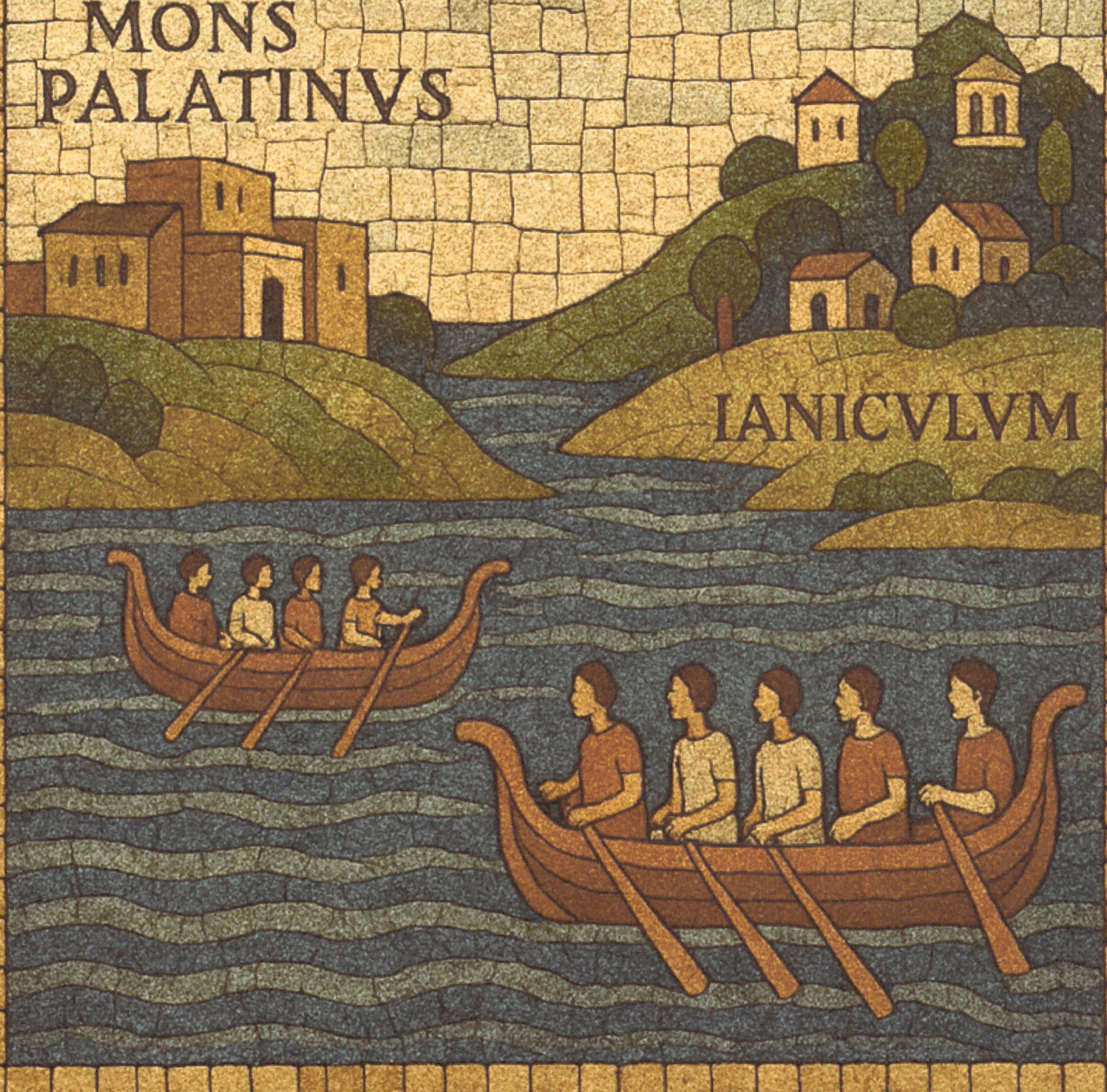

Ancus gave a command: a bridge must be built across the Tiber.

But in ancient times, the river was seen as a living god. The priests warned that a bridge might anger the river god. So they offered sacrifices to Father Tiber and prayed for peace.

They used only wood. No iron was allowed, not even nails. The bridge had to be light and sacred. It was called the Pons Sublicius, the bridge built on wooden piles.

When it was finished, Rome was joined from bank to bank for the first time.

Ancus fortified the Janiculum Hill with walls and towers. Signal fires were set to burn through the night, guarding Rome's western approach.

He also built the city's first prison. It stood in the center of Rome, meant to strike fear into the bold and lawless. The prison was called the Tullianum. It was a dark chamber carved from stone, like a deep cistern. Prisoners were lowered into it by rope and held there in silence.

They waited for trial or for execution. This place was not for mercy. It was a warning.

Ancus looked to the west, where the Tiber flowed into the sea. He knew that Rome must not only hold the land—it must reach the salt and the ships.

So he marched to the river's mouth and founded a new city. It was called Ostia, the port of Rome.

There he built docks for trading ships, salt pans for preserving food, and storehouses for the city's grain. Rome was now open to the sea.

With Ostia, Ancus gave Rome a gateway to the wider world—and the strength to grow beyond her walls.

The people of Rome came from many places. Some were born within its walls. Others had once fought against it.

Their cities had fallen, but their lives were spared. Ancus brought them into Rome and settled them on its hills. He gave them Roman laws and made them part of its growing strength.

They worshiped at Roman temples and lived by Roman ways. They were no longer enemies. They were Romans now.

Rome was no longer just a tribe. It had become something greater.

The people spoke of Ancus with praise.

The priests said, "He has restored the rites."
The soldiers said, "He has led us to victory."
The merchants said, "He has opened the sea."
The builders said, "He has made the city strong."

Ancus sought honor through lasting work: temples, laws, and victories that pleased the gods and strengthened the people.

He was called a peacemaker, a lawgiver, and a builder of lasting things. And under his reign, Rome stood firm.

When Ancus grew old, he would rise early and walk alone across the bridge.

He looked out over the river, the hills, and the harbor he had built. He saw temples where prayers were offered, soldiers guarding the walls, and ships waiting at the docks.

He prayed quietly: that Rome would remain faithful, just, and strong.

"This bridge," he thought, "joins more than land to land. It joins the peace of Numa with the power of Tullus. It holds the city together."

Ancus Marcius died after twenty-four years as king. There were no great parades, no shouting crowds. The people mourned him in quiet reverence.

They remembered him not for riches or power, but for what he had built: temples and walls, a harbor and a city, and the first bridge across the Tiber.

Long after he was gone, the people still crossed the Pons Sublicius. And as they did, they remembered the king who had joined strength with piety, and bound Rome together.

This dark stone chamber is the Tullianum, the ancient prison built by King Ancus Marcius nearly 2,700 years ago. Carved into the slope of the Capitoline Hill, it was the first prison in Rome. You can still visit it today in Rome. Long after Ancus's time, Saints Peter and Paul were imprisoned here before their martyrdom.

www.ingramcontent.com/pod-product-compliance
Lightning Source LLC
LaVergne TN
LVHW072105070426
835508LV00003B/273